I0820917

WEIRD WORLD

WEIRD SPORTS

BY CHARLIE BEATTIE

Core Library

An Imprint of Abdo Publishing
abdobooks.com

Cover image: Wife-carrying races are held annually in places such as the United States, the United Kingdom, and Finland.

abdobooks.com

Published by Abdo Publishing, a division of ABDO, PO Box 398166, Minneapolis, Minnesota 55439.

Printed in the United States of America, North Mankato, Minnesota.
102025
012026

Cover Photo: Isabel Infantes/Anadolu Agency/Getty Images
Interior Photos: Joseph Prezioso/AFP/Getty Images, 4–5; Shannon Morris/The AGE/Fairfax Media/Getty Images, 8; Alexander Welscher/dpa/picture alliance/Getty Images, 10; Gari Garaialde/AFP/Getty Images, 12–13; Anne-Christine Poujoulat/AFP/Getty Images, 14; Timur Matahari/AFP/Getty Images, 16; Shutterstock Images, 20–21, 24, 29 (top), 29 (top middle), 29 (bottom middle), 29 (bottom), 43; Johnny Green/PA Images/Getty Images, 26–27, 45; Alexi J. Rosenfeld/Getty Images News/Getty Images, 31; DozoDomo/Flickr, 34–35; Ramon Costa/SOPA Images/LightRocket/Getty Images, 37; Red Line Editorial, 40

Editor: Riley Madsen
Series Designer: Marley Richmond

Library of Congress Control Number: 2025939168

Publisher's Cataloging-in-Publication Data

Names: Beattie, Charlie, author.
Title: Weird sports / by Charlie Beattie
Description: Minneapolis, Minnesota: Abdo Publishing, 2026 | Series: Weird world | Includes online resources and index.
Identifiers: ISBN 9781098298500 (lib. bdg.) | ISBN 9798384932307 (ebook)
Subjects: LCSH: Oddities--Juvenile literature. | Sports--Juvenile literature. | Sports in popular culture--Juvenile literature. | Recreations--Juvenile literature. | Games--Juvenile literature. | Extreme sports--Juvenile literature. | Curiosities and wonders--Juvenile literature.
Classification: DDC 796.0--dc23

CONTENTS

CHAPTER ONE
Strange Races 4

CHAPTER TWO
Squad Goals 12

CHAPTER THREE
Net Games 20

CHAPTER FOUR
Everyday Sports 26

CHAPTER FIVE
Local Traditions 34

Fast Facts 42
Stop and Think 44
Glossary 46
Online Resources 47
Learn More 47
Index 48
About the Author 48

93

STRANGE RACES

On a sunny, windy October day, two men stand at the starting line for a bizarre race. After a countdown of "Three . . . two . . . one . . . go!" both men take off. The competitors have to navigate an uneven 834-foot (254 m) racecourse. At one point, they must climb over a log rail. Later in the course is a sand trap obstacle. And they must do all of it while carrying their wives on their backs.

The couples are competing in the North American Wife Carrying Championship. This race

The North American Wife Carrying Championship includes a water obstacle.

THE LEGEND BEHIND WIFE CARRYING

The sport of wife carrying comes from a Finnish legend about a man named Herkko Rosvo-Ronkainen. Known as "Ronkainen the Robber," he led a group of bandits and trained them to carry heavy loads by carrying sacks of grain. Ronkainen and his men would then go from town to town stealing grain. They sometimes kidnapped wives of people in the towns, carrying them away on their backs.

takes place every year at the Sunday River Ski Resort in Newry, Maine. The winning couple takes home a sum of money equivalent to five times the wife's weight.

The Sunday River race is one of many around the world. The Wife-Carrying World Championships are held every year in Sonkajärvi, Finland. While those who compete at Sonkajärvi are trying to win, the sport is famously laid-back. Many competitors at the 2024 Sunday River race came dressed as movie characters. Wade Porterfield and his wife, Sara, came dressed as characters from *Shrek*. Norm Koch was Mr. Incredible from *The Incredibles.* The first rule is to have fun, and the rest of the rules are fairly relaxed. Though the sport is called wife carrying, no rule says the competitors have to be married. Wives can carry husbands. And there is no rule that says the teams have to be of different genders.

A WEIRD WORLD OF SPORTS

Odd sports are played all over the globe. Some are national traditions. Others are specific to small towns. Some activities take an existing popular sport and add unique twists. Still others are the bizarre creations of imagination and invention.

Wife carrying is just one of many strange competitions. Each year, contestants gather in Virginia City, Nevada, for the World Championship Outhouse Races. Billed as the "World's Looniest Race," competitors carry outhouses they've designed themselves down the city's main street.

Other racing events bring unique challenges. At the Puffing Billy Running Festival in Australia, racers

During the half-marathon at the Puffing Billy Running Festival, runners cross train tracks at six different points.

can run distances between 0.75 miles (1.2 km) and a half-marathon. That distance is 13.1 miles (21.1 km). The trick in the half-marathon is that racers compete against Puffing Billy, a legendary locomotive engine.

ON THE WATER

Not all odd racing sports take place on land. Beginning in 1973, Portland, Oregon, has staged the annual Royal Rosarian Milk Carton Boat Race. Racers build their own boats entirely out of milk cartons. Many design them with unique artistic flourishes. The boats are powered by teams of two or four racers. After the race is completed, a local dairy calculates the amount of milk cartons used to create the winning entries. The dairy then donates the equivalent amount of milk to a Portland food bank.

BATHTUBBING

Nanaimo, Canada, is home to the annual Nanaimo-Vancouver World Championship Bathtub Race. Also known as bathtubbing, the sport is similar to the Royal Rosarian Milk Carton Boat Race. Contestants race in what look like small boats that are made from bathtub molds. The winning contestant is the first to ring a brass bell 525 feet (160 m) away from the starting line. The first tub that sinks during the race also wins a prize.

Contestants in one milk carton race in Latvia constructed an island-shaped boat with a palm tree.

The Portland race is not the only milk carton race in the world. One of the biggest races happens every year in Perth, Australia. The Masters Milk Carton Regatta is cohosted by a local dairy and a radio station. Each competitor is given 500 milk cartons to start with. They can add more of their own. Winners of the three races receive $1,000, but even bigger prizes are awarded for the most creative designs. The top design wins $5,000. Second place receives $3,000, and third gets $2,000.

STRAIGHT TO THE SOURCE

Kalob Bowman and his wife, Jenna, won gold medals in the 2024 Wife-Carrying World Championships in Finland. This race includes a run through a pond. Afterward, Kalob spoke to a journalist about the spirit of the race:

> *There's a lot of strength, there's a lot of determination and coordination that goes in with the wife that's being carried. She's upside down on your back. Her whole head simmered underwater, and it's pretty stressful. . . . It's a fun way to do something with your spouse you normally wouldn't do. It takes you out of your comfort zone and it's a fun atmosphere. There are these races all over the place . . . so find one that works for you and give it a try.*

Source: Judy Kernen. "East Valley Couples Triumph in Wife-Carrying Contest." *Ahwatukee Foothills News*, 4 Sept. 2024, ahwatukee.com. Accessed 18 June 2025.

CONSIDER YOUR AUDIENCE

Adapt this passage for a different audience, such as your friends. Write a blog post conveying this same information for the new audience. How does your post differ from the original text and why?

CHAPTER TWO

SQUAD GOALS

Sports fans are no strangers to games played with nets. Hockey is popular in cold-weather countries, and soccer is the top sport in nearly every nation on Earth. But people have created many variations of these popular games. Unicycle hockey players, for example, slap a tennis ball around while maintaining their balance on the one-wheeled vehicles.

Underwater hockey takes the sport to an even greater extreme. In the 1950s, the British Navy needed a way to train commandos and divers.

Some unicycle hockey leagues use old tennis balls because they are less bouncy.

Unlike some ice hockey leagues, underwater hockey is a noncontact sport.

In certain situations, these soldiers would have to hold their breath for extremely long periods of time. Officers decided that taking hockey underwater might be a good way for soldiers to train.

Ever since, the sport of underwater hockey has grown tremendously. The sport, which is also called Octopush, is played in at least 40 countries. It is recognized by the International Olympic Committee (IOC). Australia hosted the 2023 Underwater Hockey World Championships. The nine-day event took place in late July.

The sport is played in a pool ranging from 6 feet (1.8 m) to 13 feet (4 m) deep. The puck stays on the bottom of the pool. The six players on each team wear snorkel masks and flippers, and players frequently surface to breathe. Each player pushes the puck with a small stick. Just like regular ice or field hockey, the team with the most goals wins. But no goalies play on the teams. Teammates must work together to defend their goal, which is a small trough placed at each end of the pool.

ROSSALL HOCKEY

Each spring during the Christian observance of Lent, the Rossall School in Lancashire, England, plays its own unique adaptation of rugby and hockey. The game dates back to the mid-1800s. Because the local rugby fields were too muddy to use, they moved the game to the local beach and added sticks. Players draw a field one mile (1.6 km) long in the sand using their sticks. Two teams battle through brutal physical contact to try and push a ball into the opposing goal.

SEPAK BOLA API

Each year in Indonesia, students gather for a soccer game unlike

Sepak Bola Api is usually played at night.

any other. They play to celebrate the beginning of the Islamic holy month of Ramadan. Before taking the field, the players purify themselves with water. They then pray for a good game free of injuries. Fireworks are set off, and the game begins. The players shoot, pass, and trap the ball just like in a regular soccer game. Goalkeepers catch the ball with their hands. But they don't hold on to it for very long, because the ball is on fire.

This incredible soccer adaptation is called *Sepak Bola Api*, which translates to "flaming ball." The sport is played with a ball made of woven coconut fibers. The ball is dipped in kerosene and set alight. Before the game, players soak their feet in salt and nonflammable herbs to reduce the chance of injury.

THREE-SIDED SOCCER

Another wild adaptation of soccer involves adding more teams. In 1962, Danish artist Asger Jorn created three-sided football. In many countries, soccer is called football. Instead of a rectangular field, Jorn visualized a hexagon divided into three sections. Each section had a goal, and three teams competed against each other. The object is not to score the most goals but to give up the fewest. This allowed the teams that fell behind to work together to defeat the third team. Teams can also double-cross opponents, pretending to team up to trick the opponent into leaving its goal undefended for a moment. The double-crossing team can then sneak

FOUR-SIDED SOCCER

Each summer, one of the wildest soccer matches takes place in Florence, Italy. Four teams compete as part of a summer festival celebrating the city's rich history. All four teams play at the same time, forming what locals call *Calcio Storico Fiorentino*, which translates to "Historic Florentine Soccer." Despite having "soccer" in the name, the game is closer to rugby and is also incredibly violent. Competitors are allowed to tackle, punch, and kick each other during play. Traditionally, the winning team received a calf as a prize. Today, the team gets free dinner at a restaurant instead.

in a quick goal. Mark Dyson, who helped popularize the game in England in the 2000s, described it as a combination of soccer, chess, and poker.

Though Jorn invented the game in the 1960s, the first three-sided soccer game wasn't played until 1994. The sport has grown since then. In 2014, the first three-sided World Cup was held in Silkeborg, Denmark. That was Jorn's hometown.

STRAIGHT TO THE SOURCE

Choosing when to work with another team and when to double-cross is a big part of three-sided soccer strategy. It also makes the game unpredictable and exciting. Italian sportswriter Filippo Ricci says:

> *It is organized confusion. You can betray someone but they are not disappointed because they know it is part of the game and that the person who betrayed them could become their friend again. This makes this [soccer] very entertaining and strategic.*

Source: Sachin Nakrani. "Three-Sided Football Gives Players Something to Think About." *Guardian*, 7 May 2013, theguardian.com. Accessed 20 May 2025.

BACK IT UP

The author of this passage is using evidence to support a point. Write a paragraph describing the point the author is making. Then write down two or three pieces of evidence the author uses to make the point.

WINDSOR
BOSSABALL
TRAMPOLINES
OSSABALL
BOSSABALL

CHAPTER THREE

NET GAMES

Music producer Filip Eyckmans moved from his native Belgium to Brazil in the early 2000s. He was inspired by kids playing soccer in the streets of Rio de Janeiro. He also loved watching people playing a volleyball-soccer hybrid at the beach, as well as a Brazilian dance style and martial art called *capoeira*. Eyckmans took all of these influences, plus his childhood love of gymnastics, and created a new sport. He called it bossaball.

Bossaball's name comes from bossa nova, a Brazilian genre of music.

JOLLEYBALL

Jolleyball is a combination of volleyball and juggling. Teams of two or three players try to get a ball to land on their opponents' side of the court. But each player must also juggle two balls at all times. When the extra ball comes their way, they must juggle all three balls. A player can catch the ball three times before passing to a teammate or throwing the extra ball over the net.

Bossaball is played on what looks like a volleyball court. A center net separates two teams. But the court's surface is inflated, much like a bouncy castle. On each side of the net are trampolines. Eyckmans wanted players to use the trampolines to jump high, perform tricks, and express themselves artistically as they play. Each team gets five touches of the ball on their side, two more than the traditional number in volleyball. But one of those touches must be a soccer play such as kicking or heading the ball. The object is to set up the central player, who is bouncing on the trampoline, to score a shot over the elevated net.

The sport grew quickly after Eyckmans brought bossaball to Europe. At the 2016 Olympics in Rio de Janeiro, bossaball was set up as a demonstration sport. No official medals were awarded, but international teams competed on a court set up on the city's famous Copacabana Beach. The Netherlands took home the unofficial gold medal. Anyone interested could stop by and watch the best bossaball players in the world while listening to traditional Brazilian music. Eyckmans, true to his background as a music producer, made sure that a live band played courtside.

SEPAK TAKRAW

While bossaball is one of the newest variations on volleyball, one Southeast Asian version has been around since the 1400s. Many of the rules of *Sepak Takraw* are similar to volleyball. Each team gets three touches to get the ball over the net. Matches are played in sets, and the first team to win two out of three sets takes the match.

Sepak Takraw balls are made out of plastic or woven rattan, a flexible plant material.

However, one important difference sets the two sports apart. Volleyball players must play the ball with their hands. But in *Sepak Takraw*, players use everything but their hands. Players may use their heads, shoulders, and chest to play or control the ball, but they mainly use their feet. *Sepak Takraw* players combine soccer-like skills with acrobatic flipping moves to score points.

Sepak Takraw can be played in teams of two or three players. A three-player team is known as *regu*, which is the Malay word for "team." The three roles available to players are the server, the killer or striker, and the setter, which is also called the feeder.

The two-player version of the game is called doubles *regu*. The court is roughly the size of a badminton court. It measures 44 feet (13 m) by 20 feet (6 m).

The sport is very popular in many Asian countries. It is the national sport of Malaysia, where it's called *Sepak Raga*. Versions of *Sepak Takraw* are also played in Thailand, Myanmar, and Singapore. The sport has been part of the Asian Games sports event since 1990. In 2011, the first Sepak Takraw World Cup was held for both men and women in Kuala Lumpur, Malaysia.

TWO-HANDED TENNIS

In 2009, New York physics professor Don Mueller tried to drum up support for two-handed tennis. Mueller, who is ambidextrous, played traditional tennis with a racket in each hand. He called it a safer alternative to traditional tennis because it reduces the stress on a player's dominant hand. Tennis authorities dismissed his sport as a gimmick. And while Mueller's game briefly caught on in Russia, few players in his home country took the sport seriously.

EVERYDAY SPORTS

One day in 1997, Phil Shaw of Leicester, England, came home from a hard day of work at a local factory. Shaw had a lot of housework to do, including ironing clothes. But he wanted to go rock climbing instead. Not wanting to ignore his chores, Shaw decided to combine them with fun. He took his ironing board to the rock face, and the sport of extreme ironing was born.

Five years after Shaw's adventurous ironing escapade, the first Extreme Ironing Championships

At the first extreme ironing championships, contestants ironed in five different sections: forest, water, rocky, urban, and freestyle.

were held near Munich, Germany. Contestants had to complete an obstacle course while ironing shirts and towels. The various obstacles included lugging an ironing board into a rapidly moving river, hanging from a tree, and climbing a human-made climbing wall. Contestants weren't only judged on their speed. In order to win, they also had to make sure their clothes were as pressed as possible.

Since those beginnings, ironers have demonstrated the sport in various dangerous locations. Some have mimed the act of ironing while underwater. A group of thrill-seekers suspended themselves across the 98-foot (30-m) gorge of South Africa's Wolfberg Cracks and ironed a shirt. A group of British climbers ironed a Union Jack flag at their Mount Everest base camp in 2003.

EVERYDAY COMPETITION

Extreme ironing is just one of many everyday activities that have been turned into sports. Competitive eating contests are popular all over the world. They range

EXTREME PLACES WHERE PEOPLE
HAVE IRONED

This infographic displays some of the extreme places where people have ironed. Can you think of other extreme places where a person could iron clothes?

CURLING WITH CARS

Insurance agent Galina Kirkach lived in an icy region of Russia and witnessed a lot of accidents on slick roads. In 2017, she decided to turn what she saw into a sport. Taking inspiration from Olympic curling, Kirkach invented car curling. Instead of pushing stones across the ice, competitors push cars. One teammate stays at the wheel to steer the sliding vehicle. The goal is to move a skidding car as close to the target as possible.

from small events at carnivals and fairs to the world-famous Nathan's Hot Dog Eating Contest, which takes place every year on July 4 at Coney Island in New York City. This competition to eat as many hot dogs as possible in ten minutes was first held in 1972. It gained greater fame in 2001 when Japanese competitor Takeru Kobayashi ate a record 50 hot dogs, nearly doubling the previous record. He broke that record twice while winning the event every year until 2006.

American Joey Chestnut has dominated the sport in the two decades since. He won the event 16 times

In his 2023 Nathan's Hot Dog Eating Contest win, Joey Chestnut, *left*, ate 62 hot dogs.

between 2007 and 2023. In 2021, he wolfed down a record 76 hot dogs.

CHESSBOXING

The strategy of many sports is often compared to a chess match. Boxing is one such sport, as competitors strategically move around the ring looking for an

QUADBALL

A bizarre sport was born from one of the most popular book and movie franchises of all time. Quidditch was introduced in the first *Harry Potter* book, released in 1997. The book was later made into a 2001 movie. In 2005, a group of students at Middlebury College in Vermont adapted the game for real life. They later called it Quadball. In the books, the wizards of Hogwarts fly on brooms. In the real-life version, players run along the ground while holding PVC pipes between their legs. In the two decades since it was born at Middlebury, Quadball has spread to more than 40 countries.

opportunity to attack their opponent.

In 2003, Dutch performance artist and athlete Iepe Rubingh decided to combine boxing and chess. In chessboxing, competitors first play a round of blitz chess, a rapid, timed version of the game. Unless one of the players wins by a checkmate during the chess round, they then step into the ring for a round of boxing. The players continue to alternate until one either achieves a chess checkmate or a boxing knockout.

Rubingh won the first Chessboxing World Championship in 2003. He beat Jean Louis Veenstra in the eleventh round when Veenstra went over the chess time limit. The sport has grown slowly since then. The World Chess Boxing Organization, based in Berlin, Germany, oversees the sport and its champions.

FURTHER EVIDENCE

Chapter Four provides information about competitive eating. What is the main point of this chapter? What key evidence supports this point? Go to the article about competitive eating at the website below. Find a quote from the article that supports the chapter's main point.

SHOULD EATING COMPETITIONS BE BANNED?

abdocorelibrary.com/weird-sports

LOCAL TRADITIONS

Many sports began as local traditions before spreading to other towns, regions, and countries. While famous sports such as basketball and baseball have grown from local games into popular international sports, other games have stayed local and are not widely known. But they remain beloved in the locations in which they were born.

In Japan, players compete in the rugged game of *Bo-taoshi*. Two teams of 150 players each stand across from each other in a field.

***Bo-taoshi* towers are about 10 to 16 feet (3–4.9 m) tall.**

FINGER PULLING

Athletes compete in a strange and painful competition each year in the Alpine region of southern Germany. The town of Garmisch-Partenkirchen hosts the *fingerhakeln*, or annual "finger pulling," championships. Contestants sit across from each other at a table and hook their middle fingers together in a leather band. The competitor who pulls his or her opponent across the table wins. The sport began in the 1600s as a way to settle arguments.

The teams are divided into 75 attackers and 75 defenders. The defensive players from each team huddle around their team's tall pole. When the game begins, the attackers from each team charge at the opposing defenders. The attackers' aim is to pull down the other team's pole first. With 150 players slamming into each other around each pole, the game is violent. Players suffer bumps and bruises as opponents tackle, punch, and even kick them. The first team to bring down the opposing team's pole wins.

While *Bo-taoshi* players are focused on toppling something, *Castell* participants in Catalonia, Spain,

Castell participants typically wear clothing of the same color.

focus on building something. The goal of the game, which dates back to the early 1700s, is for a team of players to create the tallest human tower possible. Once every person in the tower is in place, a final teammate, called an *enxaneta*, climbs to the top. The *enxaneta* then raises one arm in the air to signal that the tower is complete. The *enxaneta* then scrambles down the other side of the tower. Once the *enxaneta* has made it back to the ground, the teammates in the tower disassemble. Teams are judged on the complexity, height, and creativity of their towers.

THE HENLEY ON TODD REGATTA

The annual Henley Royal Regatta is a prestigious boat race held every year on the Thames River in England. Racers in Alice Springs, Australia, have their own version, the Henley on Todd Regatta. The race is held each year on the Todd River, but there's a catch. The Todd is in the middle of Australia's legendary Outback Desert. This desert area rarely has enough water for boats to float. Instead, competitors cut the bottoms out of makeshift boats and race by running along the dry riverbed.

BRITISH TRADITIONS

Few regions of the world have more strange sports than the United Kingdom. Small towns across the country boast many unique traditions. Each year in the western English village of Brockworth, competitors gather at the top of Cooper's Hill. A large wheel of Double Gloucester cheese is then released down the steep 600-foot (180 m) hill. The contestants charge after it, often tumbling over each other. The winner is the first to get his or her hands on the cheese. No one knows exactly how long the annual tradition has been practiced. It was first written about in 1826, but research suggests it dates back hundreds of years.

Across the border from Brockworth in Llanwrtyd Wells, Wales, competitors take part in bog snorkeling. Race organizers cut a 60-yard (55 m) trench through a peat bog. Racers must wear a snorkel mask and flippers. They swim through the trench as quickly as possible, but must use only their flippers to propel themselves. They cannot use traditional swimming strokes.

The first race was organized in 1976. In 1988, Llanwrtyd Wells hosted the first Bog Snorkeling World Championships. The sport has since spread to Australia, Ireland, and Sweden.

OVER THE WATER

While contestants in Wales dive into the water, athletes in the Netherlands have created a sport by leaping over water. The country is filled with canals. Throughout the nation's history, farmers have had to navigate the

WEIRD SPORTS AROUND THE WORLD

1. Japan: *Bo-taoshi*
2. Alice Springs, Australia: Henley on Todd Regatta
3. Brockworth, England: Cooper's Hill Cheese Roll
4. Garmisch-Partenkirchen, Germany: *Fingerhakeln* World Championships
5. Llanwrtyd Wells, Wales: Bog Snorkeling World Championships
6. Catalonia, Spain: *Castell*

This map of the world shows where many weird sports were born. Are there any regions with no unusual sports noted? With some research, can you find more birthplaces of weird sports to fill in the map?

maze of waterways, many of which had no bridges. They created what is called *fierljeppen*, which means "far leaping."

When farmers needed to cross the water, they would sprint up to the water with a pole. They would plant the pole at the bottom of the canal and use the pole to propel themselves over the water to a safe landing on the other side. What began as a practical way to get around became a sport in the late 1700s. By the mid-1900s it was an organized game complete with annual world championships. Competitors are judged on their distance. Dutchman Jaco de Groot set a new mark by leaping 72 feet, 10 inches (22.2 m) in 2017.

EXPLORE ONLINE

Chapter Five discusses sports that are unique to certain towns or countries. This article explores other unusual sports. As you know, every source is different. How is the information from the website the same as the information in Chapter 5? What new information did you learn from the website?

10 UNUSUAL SPORTS

abdocorelibrary.com/weird-sports

FAST FACTS

- The North American Wife Carrying Championships take place each year in Newry, Maine.
- Competitors in milk carton races compete to finish first but are also judged by the creativity of their boat designs.
- Underwater hockey was first created by the British Navy as a way to train commandos and divers.
- In Indonesia, people play *Sepak Bola Api* to celebrate the beginning of Ramadan.
- Three-sided soccer was created by Danish artist Asger Jorn in 1962.
- Bossaball combines volleyball, soccer, gymnastics, and a Brazilian martial art known as *capoeira*.
- *Sepak Takraw* is the national sport of Malaysia, where it is known as *Sepak Raga*.
- Phil Shaw invented extreme ironing in Leicester, England, in 1997.

- Dutch artist and boxer Iepe Rubingh created chessboxing in 2003 and won the sport's first world championship that same year.
- *Castell*-building teams compete to create elaborate human towers.
- *Fierljeppen* was originally a way for Dutch farmers to leap over the country's many canals. It became a sport in the 1700s.

STOP AND THINK

Dig Deeper

After reading this book, what questions do you still have about weird sports? With an adult's help, find a few reliable sources that can help you answer your questions. Write a paragraph about what you learned.

You Are There

This book discusses several sports that began in small towns in the United Kingdom. Imagine you are traveling to these events. Write a letter home telling your friends what you have found. What do you notice about the sports and their locations? Be sure to add plenty of detail to your notes.

Take a Stand

This book refers to many sports as weird. But people do not always agree on what makes a sport weird. What kinds of sports do you find weird? Why? Are there any sports mentioned in this book that you don't find weird?

Why Do I Care?

You may never have seen any weird sports in person. But that doesn't mean you can't learn more about them. Which weird sports would you like to see in person? Do you have friends or family who have seen weird sports?

GLOSSARY

adaptation
the process of changing something to fit a new environment or condition

ambidextrous
able to use both hands equally well

bandit
a thieving outlaw who usually travels in a group or gang

commando
a member of a military unit that performs raids

demonstration sport
a sport played at the Olympic Games as an exhibition, without medals awarded to the winners

equivalent
equal to

gimmick
something designed to attract attention

obstacle
something that blocks the way forward

tradition
a custom or belief that is passed from one generation to the next

ONLINE RESOURCES

To learn more about weird sports, visit our free resource websites below.

Visit **abdocorelibrary.com** or scan this QR code for free Common Core resources for teachers and students, including vetted activities, multimedia, and booklinks, for deeper subject comprehension.

Visit **abdobooklinks.com** or scan this QR code for free additional online weblinks for further learning. These links are routinely monitored and updated to provide the most current information available.

LEARN MORE

Hustad, Douglas. *Innovations in Hockey*. Abdo, 2022.

Olson, Ethan. *Ironman Triathlons*. Abdo, 2024.

INDEX

Bo-taoshi, 35–36, 40
bog snorkeling, 39, 40
bossaball, 21–23
Bowman, Kalob, 11

Calcio Storico Fiorentino, 18
capoeira, 21
Castell, 36–37, 40
chessboxing, 31–33
Chestnut, Joey, 30–31
Cooper's Hill Cheese Roll, 38–39, 40

Dyson, Mark, 18

extreme ironing, 27–29
Eyckmans, Filip, 21–23

fierljeppen, 39–41
fingerhakeln, 36, 40

Groot, Jaco de, 41

Henley on Todd Regatta, 38, 40

Jorn, Asger, 17–18

Kobayashi, Takeru, 30
Koch, Norm, 6

Masters Milk Carton Regatta, 10
Mueller, Don, 25

Nathan's Hot Dog Eating Contest, 30–31, 33

Olympics, 14, 23, 30

Porterfield, Wade, 6
Puffing Billy Running Festival, 7–8

Quadball, 32

Ricci, Filippo, 19
Rossall hockey, 15
Rosvo-Ronkainen, Herkko, 6
Royal Rosarian Milk Carton Boat Race, 9–10
Rubingh, Iepe, 32–33

Sepak Bola Api, 15–17
Sepak Takraw, 23–25
Shaw, Phil, 27

three-sided football, 17–19
two-handed tennis, 25

underwater hockey, 13–15
unicycle hockey, 13

wife carrying, 5–7, 11

About the Author

Charlie Beattie is a writer, editor, and former sportscaster. Originally from Saint Paul, Minnesota, he now lives in Charleston, South Carolina, with his wife and son.